Affirmations for Revolution

a coloring book
by Stephanie McMillan

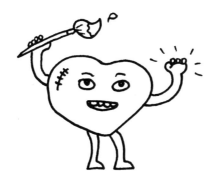

Deep thanks to the plants who feed us all.

ForwardSpiral.org
StephanieMcMillan.org

Forward Spiral
P.O. Box 460673
Fort Lauderdale, FL 33346
hello@forwardspiral.org

First edition: June 1, 2021

ISBN: 978-0-9916047-6-0

Printed in the United States of America

Color Test Page

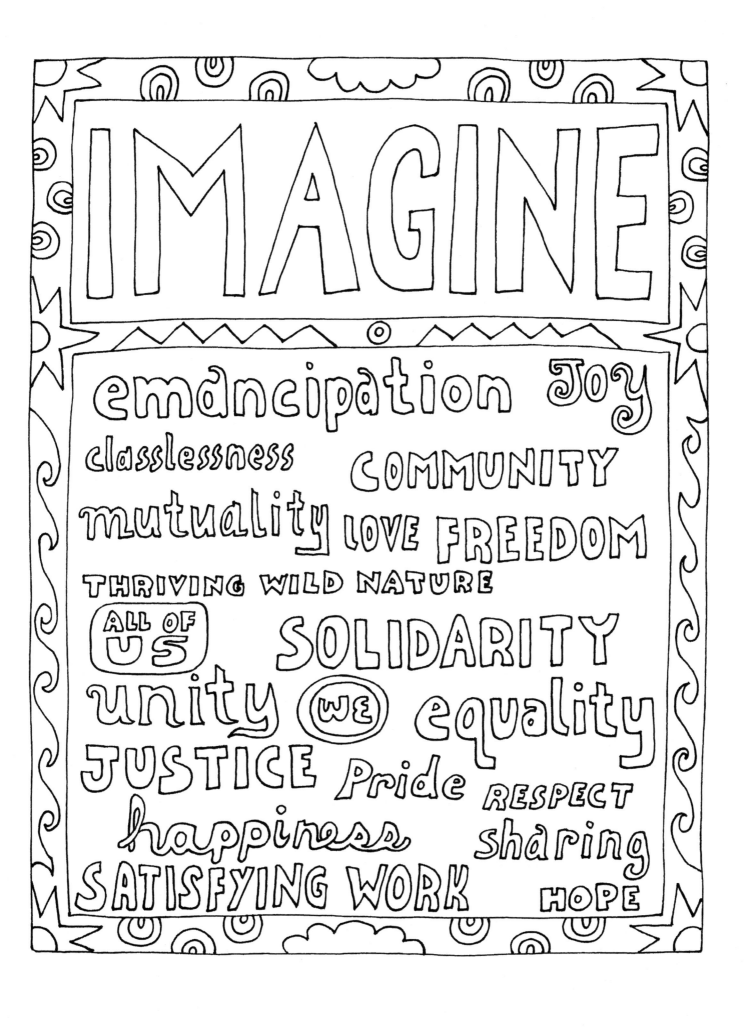

Made in United States
North Haven, CT
26 May 2024

52958182R00024